A Year of Positive Thoughts

A Daily Journal to Guide You on a Path to Motivation, Happiness, and Growth

This Book Belongs To

_____

Positive thinking is about much more than just displaying an optimistic attitude or thinking happy thoughts. Research about positive thinking has shown that positive thoughts can create a real value to your life. They can help build an emotional resource skill-set that will carry throughout your life.

Journaling about the positive things in one's life has been shown to have many beneficial effects such as stress relief, emotional well-being, success in your endeavors, and even better physical health.

The questions in this journal are designed to help you discover the positive aspects of your world and celebrate the good things in your life. You will learn about yourself and begin a journey of life change as you reflect upon the positives in your life.

Here are some tips to use this journal:

- ❖ Each page covers three questions (one page a day for three days) allowing you to record a full year of positive thoughts.

- ❖ Set aside five minutes or so every day to think about and answer one of the questions or prompts each day.

- ❖ Try to consistently write at the same time every day so that your journal writing becomes a habit. Choose a quiet place without distractions.

- ❖ Date the entry so you have a point of reference when you look back through it later.

- ❖ Add drawings or photos if you want – the more personalized it is the more effective it is.

- ❖ Be honest with yourself. No one else needs to see your journal unless you want to share it.

- ❖ There is no right or wrong answer – just write what you are thinking and feeling.

___/___ /20___

List three things that went well today.

_____

_____

_____

_____

___ /___ /20___

What have you done in your life that you are most proud of?

_____

_____

_____

_____

___ /___ /20___

What are three of your favorite movies? Why?

_____

_____

_____

_____

___/___/20___

List three people you admire? Why?

_____

_____

_____

_____

___/___/20___

List three activities you enjoy doing with your family?

_____

_____

_____

_____

___/___/20___

What makes you smile?

_____

_____

_____

_____

____ / ____ /20____

What is the best compliment you have ever received?

_____

_____

_____

_____

____ / ____ /20____

Describe the kindest thing you have done for another person.

_____

_____

_____

_____

____ / ____ /20____

List three things you are grateful for?

_____

_____

_____

_____

_____ / _____ /20_____

What is your favorite book? Why?

_____

_____

_____

_____

_____ / _____ /20_____

Describe a simple pleasure that makes you happy.

_____

_____

_____

_____

_____ / _____ /20_____

List three ways that you are awesome.

_____

_____

_____

_____

___ / ___ /20___

Describe an ideal day. What would it look like?

_____

_____

_____

_____

___ / ___ /20___

Describe something that puts you in a good mood.

_____

_____

_____

_____

___ / ___ /20___

Describe a time you stayed calm while solving a tough problem.

_____

_____

_____

_____

_____ / _____ / 20_____

Who is the most positive person you know? Why?

_____

_____

_____

_____

_____ / _____ / 20_____

What is your favorite thing about yourself? How does it impact
your life?

_____

_____

_____

_____

_____ / _____ / 20_____

What inspires you to be better? Why?

_____

_____

_____

_____

___/___/20___

Who can you turn to for advice and support?

___/___/20___

Describe the positive aspects of your home.

___/___/20___

Describe how giving gifts to your loved ones makes you feel.

_____ / _____ / 20_____

What is one negative thing you can eliminate from your life?

_____

_____

_____

_____

_____ / _____ / 20_____

Describe a fun adventure you have had.

_____

_____

_____

_____

_____ / _____ / 20_____

What would you do to cheer up your best friend?

_____

_____

_____

_____

___/___/20___

What is your favorite hobby? Why?

_____

_____

_____

_____

___/___/20___

Think of one healthy habit you could maintain to make your life better.

_____

_____

_____

_____

___/___/20___

What was the last thing that made you laugh?

_____

_____

_____

_____

___ / ___ / 20___

Finish the thought: I deserve love because...

_____

_____

_____

_____

___ / ___ / 20___

What positive character traits do you have?

_____

_____

_____

_____

___ / ___ / 20___

When do you feel most safe?

_____

_____

_____

_____

___ / ___ / 20___

What are your favorite aromas?

_____

_____

_____

_____

___ / ___ / 20___

Finish the thought: My favorite way to relax is...

_____

_____

_____

_____

___ / ___ / 20___

Describe a random act of kindness you have done for someone.

_____

_____

_____

_____

___ / ___ /20___

Describe a happy time in your childhood.

_____

_____

_____

_____

___ / ___ /20___

What is your favorite sweet treat?

_____

_____

_____

_____

___ / ___ /20___

Do you indulge yourself? How can you do it more often?

_____

_____

_____

_____

___ / ___ /20___

What is your wildest dream?

_____

_____

_____

_____

___ / ___ /20___

Finish the thought: Today I accomplished...

_____

_____

_____

_____

___ / ___ /20___

List three ways in which you are awesome.

_____

_____

_____

_____

____ / ____ /20____

Describe an important goal that you achieved.

_____

_____

_____

_____

____ / ____ /20____

What do you know how to do well?

_____

_____

_____

_____

____ / ____ /20____

What is something you can let go of to make your life better?

_____

_____

_____

_____

_____ / _____ /20_____

What would your teenage self be most proud of you for?

_____

_____

_____

_____

_____ / _____ /20_____

Describe when you stepped out of your comfort zone to accomplish something.

_____

_____

_____

_____

_____ / _____ /20_____

What is your favorite holiday? Why?

_____

_____

_____

_____

__ / __ /20__

What makes you unique?

_____

_____

_____

_____

__ / __ /20__

Write a love letter to your least favorite part of your body.

_____

_____

_____

_____

__ / __ /20__

What gift would you like to give to your best friend?

_____

_____

_____

_____

___ / ___ / 20___

What do others brag about when they describe you?

_____

_____

_____

_____

___ / ___ / 20___

Finish the thought: My favorite way to play is...

_____

_____

_____

_____

___ / ___ / 20___

What songs put you in a good mood?

_____

_____

_____

_____

___ / ___ /20___

What TV shows do you enjoy?

_____

_____

_____

_____

___ / ___ /20___

What are you good at helping others with?

_____

_____

_____

_____

___ / ___ /20___

What is your favorite restaurant? Why?

_____

_____

_____

_____

___ / ___ /20___

Finish the thought: I am most happy when I am wearing...

_____

_____

_____

_____

___ / ___ /20___

Describe three things you cannot go without.

_____

_____

_____

_____

___ / ___ /20___

Where would you most like to go on a vacation? Why?

_____

_____

_____

_____

_____ / _____ /20_____

Describe a time when a situation seemed bad but turned out well.

_____

_____

_____

_____

_____ / _____ /20_____

What can you do today to make someone else's day better?

_____

_____

_____

_____

_____ / _____ /20_____

What is the best compliment you ever gave?

_____

_____

_____

_____

_____ / _____ / 20 _____

What positive habits do you have?

_____

_____

_____

_____

_____ / _____ / 20 _____

Describe what a relaxing evening looks like.

_____

_____

_____

_____

_____ / _____ / 20 _____

List three positive statements about yourself, beginning with the phrase "I am ..."

_____

_____

_____

_____

___/___/20___

Finish the thought: I deserve joy because...

_____

_____

_____

_____

___/___/20___

Write a positive affirmation you could start every day with.

_____

_____

_____

_____

___/___/20___

Finish the thought: Today I accomplished...

_____

_____

_____

_____

_____ / _____ / 20_____

Finish the thought: Three things that bring me peace are...

_____

_____

_____

_____

_____ / _____ / 20_____

What things would you like to say 'no' to? Why don't you?

_____

_____

_____

_____

_____ / _____ / 20_____

In what situations do you feel strong?

_____

_____

_____

_____

____/____/20____

Who shows you appreciation?

_____

_____

_____

_____

____/____/20____

Who are your role models? How are you already like them?

_____

_____

_____

_____

____/____/20____

What would actually change in your life if your body was perfect?

_____

_____

_____

_____

___ / ___ / 20___

Describe three positive things about your home.

_____

_____

_____

_____

___ / ___ / 20___

Write a pep talk to give to yourself when you are sad or upset.

_____

_____

_____

_____

___ / ___ / 20___

If you made yourself a priority in your life, what would change?

_____

_____

_____

_____

___ / ___ /20___

How can having a positive attitude change your life?

_____

_____

_____

_____

___ / ___ /20___

List three quotes that inspire you.

_____

_____

_____

_____

___ / ___ /20___

What sights, sounds, tastes, and feelings do you associate with
the word 'joy'?

_____

_____

_____

_____

_____ / _____ / 20 _____

If your perfect day could contain one thing, what would it be?

_____

_____

_____

_____

_____ / _____ / 20 _____

List three places you enjoy visiting.

_____

_____

_____

_____

_____ / _____ / 20 _____

List your top three short term goals.

_____

_____

_____

_____

___ / ___ / 20___

What is your body telling you right now?

_____

_____

_____

_____

___ / ___ / 20___

What have you done that you never thought you would be able to do?

_____

_____

_____

_____

___ / ___ / 20___

List your top three long term goals.

_____

_____

_____

_____

___ /___ /20___

Describe a favorite book character. In what ways are you like him or her?

_____

_____

_____

_____

___ /___ /20___

Describe your personal style?

_____

_____

_____

_____

___ /___ /20___

What does the word friendship bring to mind?

_____

_____

_____

_____

___ / ___ /20___

List three famous lines from movies that you like.

___ / ___ /20___

What one thing would you do if you knew you could not fail?

___ / ___ /20___

What are three things you do well?

____ / ____ /20____

Describe a time when you were brave.

_____

_____

_____

_____

____ / ____ /20____

What qualities do you display that others admire?

_____

_____

_____

_____

____ / ____ /20____

What do you need to do to conquer your biggest fear?

_____

_____

_____

_____

___/___/20___

In what ways do you consider yourself quirky?

_____

_____

_____

_____

___/___/20___

Describe a time when you felt really smart.

_____

_____

_____

_____

___/___/20___

What historical person do you most admire?

_____

_____

_____

___ / ___ / 20___

What do you appreciate about your current situation?

_____

_____

_____

_____

___ / ___ / 20___

In what ways do you feel lovable?

_____

_____

_____

_____

___ / ___ / 20___

Describe a time when you acted with courage.

_____

_____

_____

_____

_____ / _____ / 20_____

What three things are you most grateful for today?

_____

_____

_____

_____

_____ / _____ / 20_____

What do you regret in life? What lessons can you take from it?

_____

_____

_____

_____

_____ / _____ / 20_____

Describe a time when you made a new beginning.

_____

_____

_____

_____

___ / ___ /20___

What do you think is your purpose in life?

_____

_____

_____

_____

___ / ___ /20___

Who in your life do you need to forgive?

_____

_____

_____

_____

___ / ___ /20___

What would you like to invent to make the world a better place?

_____

_____

_____

_____

___ / ___ /20___

How did it feel the last time you helped someone?

_____

_____

_____

_____

___ / ___ /20___

In what ways are you continuing to grow as a person?

_____

_____

_____

_____

___ / ___ /20___

What are you putting off doing? Why?

_____

_____

_____

_____

____ /____ /20____

Describe your sense of humor.

_____

_____

_____

_____

____ /____ /20____

Write a fairy tale in which you live happily ever after.

_____

_____

_____

_____

____ /____ /20____

What things in your life do you really enjoy?

_____

_____

_____

_____

___ / ___ / 20___

What made you smile today?

_____

_____

_____

_____

___ / ___ / 20___

What compliments did you receive this week?

_____

_____

_____

_____

___ / ___ / 20___

Describe yourself in twelve words?

_____

_____

_____

_____

_____ / _____ /20_____

When was the last time you cried for joy?

_____

_____

_____

_____

_____ / _____ /20_____

Who do you love?

_____

_____

_____

_____

_____ / _____ /20_____

Who would you like to give a gift to? What would it be?

_____

_____

_____

_____

_____ / _____ /20_____

What challenge did you overcome today?

_____

_____

_____

_____

_____ / _____ /20_____

What natural wonders would you like to visit?

_____

_____

_____

_____

_____ / _____ /20_____

List three ideas for stepping out of your comfort zone.

_____

_____

_____

_____

_____ / _____ /20_____

Who are three people who have helped you?

_____

_____

_____

_____

_____ / _____ /20_____

Describe your best character traits.

_____

_____

_____

_____

_____ / _____ /20_____

What is the best advice someone has given you?

_____

_____

_____

_____

_____ / _____ /20_____

What are some important goals you have achieved this year?

_____

_____

_____

_____

_____ / _____ /20_____

If you could star in a movie, what would it be?

_____

_____

_____

_____

_____ / _____ /20_____

Who is your favorite celebrity? Why?

_____

_____

_____

_____

___ / ___ /20___

How will you remind yourself today how amazing you are?

_____

_____

_____

_____

___ / ___ /20___

What can you do today that you couldn't do five years ago?

_____

_____

_____

_____

___ / ___ /20___

What warms you on a cold winter night?

_____

_____

_____

_____

___ / ___ /20___

Describe a time you taught someone something.

_____

_____

_____

_____

___ / ___ /20___

Who should play you in a movie about your life?

_____

_____

_____

_____

___ / ___ /20___

What do you like most about your current job?

_____

_____

_____

_____

_____ / _____ /20_____

Who can you turn to for good advice?

_____

_____

_____

_____

_____ / _____ /20_____

What is your favorite television comedy?

_____

_____

_____

_____

_____ / _____ /20_____

What do others often ask you to help them with?

_____

_____

_____

_____

___/___/20___

What talent do you have that others do not know about?

_____

_____

_____

_____

___/___/20___

In what ways do you display your creativity?

_____

_____

_____

_____

___/___/20___

What about yourself are you proud of?

_____

_____

_____

_____

___ / ___ / 20___

Who outside your family has had a positive impact on your life?

_____

_____

_____

_____

___ / ___ / 20___

What comfort food brightens your day?

_____

_____

_____

_____

___ / ___ / 20___

Describe a happy childhood memory.

_____

_____

_____

_____

_____ / _____ /20_____

Write a three word motto about the good in life.

_____

_____

_____

_____

_____ / _____ /20_____

What is your favorite season?

_____

_____

_____

_____

_____ / _____ /20_____

What brings you good luck?

_____

_____

_____

_____

____ / ____ / 20____

What are you looking forward to in the coming year?

_____

_____

_____

_____

____ / ____ / 20____

What is your most comfortable clothing?

_____

_____

_____

_____

____ / ____ / 20____

What made you laugh yesterday?

_____

_____

_____

_____

___/___/20___

Describe a perfect vacation.

_____

_____

_____

_____

___/___/20___

What is the nicest thing someone did for you this week?

_____

_____

_____

_____

___/___/20___

What are your top five personal principles?

_____

_____

_____

_____

___ /___ /20___

What is the best thing about where you live?

_____

_____

_____

_____

___ /___ /20___

What is the best decision you ever made?

_____

_____

_____

_____

___ /___ /20___

What do you admire most about yourself?

_____

_____

_____

_____

___ / ___ /20___

What gets you enthusiastic about life?

_____

_____

_____

_____

___ / ___ /20___

Where do you feel relaxed?

_____

_____

_____

_____

___ / ___ /20___

What can you do today to take one step toward your goal?

_____

_____

_____

_____

_____ / _____ / 20 _____

When you have an hour of free time, what will you do?

_____

_____

_____

_____

_____ / _____ / 20 _____

What do you deserve an award for?

_____

_____

_____

_____

_____ / _____ / 20 _____

What are your best leadership qualities?

_____

_____

_____

_____

_____ / _____ /20_____

What motivates you to go to work every day?

_____

_____

_____

_____

_____ / _____ /20_____

What has been your most enjoyable family activity in the last year?

_____

_____

_____

_____

_____ / _____ /20_____

What gives you a feeling of security?

_____

_____

_____

_____

_____ /_____ /20_____

What skill do you have that you rarely use?

_____

_____

_____

_____

_____ /_____ /20_____

When did you do something spontaneous?

_____

_____

_____

_____

_____ /_____ /20_____

If you were a star athlete, what sport would you compete in?

_____

_____

_____

_____

___ / ___ /20___

What food is your guilty pleasure?

_____

_____

_____

_____

___ / ___ /20___

What is your favorite sunny day activity?

_____

_____

_____

_____

___ / ___ /20___

How do you celebrate your birthday?

_____

_____

_____

_____

____ / ____ / 20____

What is your favorite drink on a hot day?

_____

_____

_____

_____

____ / ____ / 20____

Describe your funniest travel experience.

_____

_____

_____

_____

____ / ____ / 20____

What is the most comfortable piece of furniture you have?

_____

_____

_____

_____

___ / ___ /20___

What is your mission in life?

_____

_____

_____

_____

___ / ___ /20___

What do you want people to remember about you?

_____

_____

_____

_____

___ / ___ /20___

What do you daydream about?

_____

_____

_____

_____

___ / ___ /20___

What will you do this week to make the world a better place?

_____

_____

_____

_____

___ / ___ /20___

Who do you always make sure to be nice to?

_____

_____

_____

_____

___ / ___ /20___

What was better about today than yesterday?

_____

_____

_____

_____

_____ / _____ / 20_____

Who in your life can you rely on?

_____

_____

_____

_____

_____ / _____ / 20_____

In what ways are you beautiful?

_____

_____

_____

_____

_____ / _____ / 20_____

What is the biggest opportunity in your life right now?

_____

_____

_____

_____

_____ / _____ / 20_____

Describe a time when the impossible became possible.

_____

_____

_____

_____

_____ / _____ / 20_____

What makes you feel appreciated?

_____

_____

_____

_____

_____ / _____ / 20_____

Finish the thought: The happiest time in my life was...

_____

_____

_____

_____

___ / ___ /20___

What are the components of a happy life?

_____

_____

_____

_____

___ / ___ /20___

When have you overcome your fears and done it anyway?

_____

_____

_____

_____

___ / ___ /20___

How do you celebrate your successes?

_____

_____

_____

_____

___ / ___ /20___

What activity makes you lose track of time?

_____

_____

_____

_____

___ / ___ /20___

What do you think stands between you and happiness?

_____

_____

_____

_____

___ / ___ /20___

What do you see when you close your eyes?

_____

_____

_____

_____

___ / ___ /20___

What will matter to you most when you are 80 years old?

_____

_____

_____

_____

___ / ___ /20___

What do you have that you can live without?

_____

_____

_____

_____

___ / ___ /20___

When do you feel most peaceful?

_____

_____

_____

_____

___ /___ /20___

Who or what do you think of when you think of love?

_____

_____

_____

_____

___ /___ /20___

If you could relive one day in your live, what day would it be?

_____

_____

_____

_____

___ /___ /20___

What is your definition of heaven?

_____

_____

_____

_____

___ / ___ / 20___

If you were granted one wish, what would it be?

_____

_____

_____

_____

___ / ___ / 20___

What do you have that money cannot buy?

_____

_____

_____

_____

___ / ___ / 20___

What possession makes you most happy?

_____

_____

_____

_____

___ / ___ /20___

When have you worked hard and enjoyed every minute?

_____

_____

_____

_____

___ / ___ /20___

What have you done recently to help someone else?

_____

_____

_____

_____

___ / ___ /20___

What are you looking forward to?

_____

_____

_____

_____

___ / ___ /20___

How are you pursuing your dreams right now?

_____

_____

_____

_____

___ / ___ /20___

What skills did you display this week?

_____

_____

_____

_____

___ / ___ /20___

What makes a happy life?

_____

_____

_____

_____

___ / ___ /20___

What have you learned recently that changed your attitude?

_____

_____

_____

_____

___ / ___ /20___

Imagine a relaxing afternoon. What are you doing?

_____

_____

_____

_____

___ / ___ /20___

What is the best part of growing older?

_____

_____

_____

_____

___ / ___ /20___

What are your top three priorities right now?

_____

_____

_____

_____

___ / ___ /20___

What book has had the greatest influence on your life?

_____

_____

_____

_____

___ / ___ /20___

What do you think is worth waiting for?

_____

_____

_____

_____

___/___/20___

What is your greatest strength?

_____

_____

_____

_____

___/___/20___

What will you never give up on?

_____

_____

_____

_____

___/___/20___

What motivates you to give your all?

_____

_____

_____

_____

___ / ___ / 20___

What made you smile this week?

_____

_____

_____

_____

___ / ___ / 20___

What new experiences are you looking forward to enjoying?

_____

_____

_____

_____

___ / ___ / 20___

What is one action you can take to move forward in life?

_____

_____

_____

_____

_____ / _____ / 20 _____

What do you do to relieve stress?

_____

_____

_____

_____

_____ / _____ / 20 _____

What is your favorite true story that you share with others?

_____

_____

_____

_____

_____ / _____ / 20 _____

What was your latest major accomplishment?

_____

_____

_____

_____

___ / ___ / 20___

What is the best choice you ever made?

_____

_____

_____

_____

___ / ___ / 20___

What is the most important lesson you learned in the last year?

_____

_____

_____

_____

___ / ___ / 20___

What current distraction can you rid yourself of?

_____

_____

_____

_____

_____ / _____ /20_____

Who in your life has been there for you?

_____

_____

_____

_____

_____ / _____ /20_____

What is something most people don't know about you?

_____

_____

_____

_____

_____ / _____ /20_____

Whose life have you had the greatest impact on?

_____

_____

_____

_____

____ / ____ /20____

What are you excited about right now?

_____

_____

_____

_____

____ / ____ /20____

What is the biggest change you made in the last year?

_____

_____

_____

_____

____ / ____ /20____

What is the best recommendation you ever received?

_____

_____

_____

_____

___ / ___ /20___

Where will you go on your dream vacation?

_____

_____

_____

_____

___ / ___ /20___

What do you admire most about your parents?

_____

_____

_____

_____

___ / ___ /20___

What makes you feel good about yourself?

_____

_____

_____

_____

___ / ___ / 20___

What is the one main quality you look for in a partner?

_____

_____

_____

_____

___ / ___ / 20___

If you could be someone else for a day, who would you be? Why?

_____

_____

_____

_____

___ / ___ / 20___

In what ways are you amazing?

_____

_____

_____

_____

___ / ___ / 20 ___

What is your favorite sound?

_____

_____

_____

_____

___ / ___ / 20 ___

What is your number one source of motivation right now?

_____

_____

_____

_____

___ / ___ / 20 ___

Who was the last person you said 'I love you' to?

_____

_____

_____

_____

_____ / _____ /20_____

What are the top three qualities you look for in a friend?

_____

_____

_____

_____

_____ / _____ /20_____

What music do you listen to that lifts your spirits?

_____

_____

_____

_____

_____ / _____ /20_____

What specific character trait do you want to be known for?

_____

_____

_____

_____

_____ / _____ / 20_____

What did you do this past year that is memorable?

_____

_____

_____

_____

_____ / _____ / 20_____

What is something you wish you had done earlier in life?

_____

_____

_____

_____

_____ / _____ / 20_____

What do you know well enough to teach others?

_____

_____

_____

_____

___ / ___ /20___

What is your favorite time of the day? Why?

_____

_____

_____

_____

___ / ___ /20___

Who is your favorite fictional hero or heroine?

_____

_____

_____

_____

___ / ___ /20___

What is your favorite animal? Why?

_____

_____

_____

_____

___ / ___ /20___

What is your best holiday memory?

_____

_____

_____

_____

___ / ___ /20___

What is the most unusual place you have ever been?

_____

_____

_____

_____

___ / ___ /20___

What is your best personality trait?

_____

_____

_____

_____

___/___/20___

When was the last time you felt lucky?

_____

_____

_____

_____

___/___/20___

Describe your favorite hideaway.

_____

_____

_____

_____

___/___/20___

What is your favorite store? Why?

_____

_____

_____

_____

___ / ___ /20___

When are you most productive?

_____

_____

_____

_____

___ / ___ /20___

Who was your most memorable teacher?

_____

_____

_____

_____

___ / ___ /20___

Where was the most comfortable place you ever slept?

_____

_____

_____

_____

____ / ____ /20____

Describe a time when you felt fearless.

_____

_____

_____

_____

____ / ____ /20____

What word is really fun to say?

_____

_____

_____

_____

____ / ____ /20____

What is the cutest thing you can think of?

_____

_____

_____

_____

___ / ___ /20___

What topic could you spend hours and hours talking about?

_____

_____

_____

_____

___ / ___ /20___

What always makes you cheerful when you think about it?

_____

_____

_____

_____

___ / ___ /20___

What food do you most often crave?

_____

_____

_____

_____

_____ / _____ / 20_____

What was your most physically pleasurable experience?

_____

_____

_____

_____

_____ / _____ / 20_____

What company do you most admire?

_____

_____

_____

_____

_____ / _____ / 20_____

When was the last time you complimented someone?

_____

_____

_____

_____

___ /___ /20___

What is the most pleasant sounding foreign accent?

_____

_____

_____

_____

___ /___ /20___

If you wrote a book, what would it be about?

_____

_____

_____

_____

___ /___ /20___

What topic are you interested in that many people aren't?

_____

_____

_____

_____

____ / ____ /20____

What food do you most like to prepare?

_____

_____

_____

_____

____ / ____ /20____

What really needs to be updated?

_____

_____

_____

_____

____ / ____ /20____

What is the funniest-looking animal?

_____

_____

_____

_____

_____ / _____ / 20_____

What was your most humbling experience?

_____

_____

_____

_____

_____ / _____ / 20_____

If you went to a costume party, what costume would you wear?

_____

_____

_____

_____

_____ / _____ / 20_____

Who or what should you stop making excuses for?

_____

_____

_____

_____

___ / ___ / 20___

What are you better at than you give yourself credit?

_____

_____

_____

_____

___ / ___ / 20___

When did a small success lead to a bigger success?

_____

_____

_____

_____

___ / ___ / 20___

What are you curious about?

_____

_____

_____

_____

___ / ___ / 20___

When is the last time you made someone laugh?

_____

_____

_____

_____

___ / ___ / 20___

What did you do yesterday to help someone else?

_____

_____

_____

_____

___ / ___ / 20___

Write down three things that make you special?

_____

_____

_____

_____

_____ / _____ /20_____

Describe a time when you were discouraged but persevered?

_____

_____

_____

_____

_____ / _____ /20_____

What do you visualize when you hear the word success?

_____

_____

_____

_____

_____ / _____ /20_____

What are you confident about?

_____

_____

_____

_____

___ / ___ /20___

What is something you purchased that you are excited about?

_____

_____

_____

_____

___ / ___ /20___

How do you feel after a good night's sleep?

_____

_____

_____

_____

___ / ___ /20___

Who are you proud to be associated with?

_____

_____

_____

_____

___ / ___ / 20___

What special indulgence makes you feel good?

_____

_____

_____

_____

___ / ___ / 20___

If you invented a game, what would it look like?

_____

_____

_____

_____

___ / ___ / 20___

What healthy habits do you have?

_____

_____

_____

_____

___ / ___ /20___

What non-profit would you start if you had funding?

_____

_____

_____

_____

___ / ___ /20___

What do you want to do with the rest of your life?

_____

_____

_____

_____

___ / ___ /20___

What is your most remarkable quality?

_____

_____

_____

_____

___ / ___ /20___

Describe a time when you felt blissful?

_____

_____

_____

_____

___ / ___ /20___

What are you grateful for today?

_____

_____

_____

_____

___ / ___ /20___

Write a poem about happiness.

_____

_____

_____

_____

___ / ___ / 20___

What is one action you can take tomorrow to move forward?

_____

_____

_____

_____

___ / ___ / 20___

Take five minutes to focus your attention on your breathing.

_____

_____

_____

_____

___ / ___ / 20___

If your body could talk, what would it tell you?

_____

_____

_____

_____

___ / ___ /20___

When did you display courage in the face of adversity?

_____

_____

_____

_____

___ / ___ /20___

What clothes do you wear to feel attractive?

_____

_____

_____

_____

___ / ___ /20___

What brings you peace in stressful times?

_____

_____

_____

_____

___ / ___ /20___

When is good enough better than perfect?

_____

_____

_____

_____

___ / ___ /20___

What is your favorite activity on a warm summer day?

_____

_____

_____

_____

___ / ___ /20___

Finish the thought: I deserve to be happy because...

_____

_____

_____

_____

___ / ___ /20___

What negative thought can you let go of?

_____

_____

_____

_____

___ / ___ /20___

What do you have faith in?

_____

_____

_____

_____

___ / ___ /20___

What is your favorite color? Why?

_____

_____

_____

_____

___ / ___ /20___

What is good about this time in your life?

_____

_____

_____

_____

___ / ___ /20___

What went well this week?

_____

_____

_____

_____

___ / ___ /20___

Finish the thought: I forgive myself for...

_____

_____

_____

_____

___ / ___ /20___

Describe a time when you performed well under pressure.

_____
_____
_____
_____

___ / ___ /20___

What is the most tranquil experience you can think of?

_____
_____
_____
_____

___ / ___ /20___

What are you holding on to that you no longer need?

_____
_____
_____
_____

___ / ___ /20___

When do you feel serenity?

_____

_____

_____

_____

___ / ___ /20___

What made you smile recently?

_____

_____

_____

_____

___ / ___ /20___

What do you do to soothe an aching body?

_____

_____

_____

_____

___ / ___ /20___

What emotions do you associate with confidence?

_____

_____

_____

_____

___ / ___ /20___

Who will love you no matter what?

_____

_____

_____

_____

___ / ___ /20___

Who do you think is a good leader? Why?

_____

_____

_____

_____

___ / ___ / 20___

Write a pep talk for when you feel upset about something.

_____

_____

_____

_____

___ / ___ / 20___

Looking back, list three great accomplishments in your life.

_____

_____

_____

_____

___ / ___ / 20___

What is one thing in your life you should say 'no' to?

_____

_____

_____

_____

_____ / _____ /20_____

What do you love about your life right now?

_____
_____
_____
_____

_____ / _____ /20_____

When was the last time you asked someone for help?

_____
_____
_____
_____

_____ / _____ /20_____

Can you let yourself feel happy just doing nothing?

_____
_____
_____
_____

___ / ___ / 20___

What makes you unique?

_____

_____

_____

_____

___ / ___ / 20___

Who in your life really loves and supports you?

_____

_____

_____

_____

___ / ___ / 20___

Why is asking for help a strength and not a weakness?

_____

_____

_____

_____

___/___/20___

What have you done this week to indulge yourself?

_____

_____

_____

_____

___/___/20___

Write down three inspiring quotes that give you encouragement.

_____

_____

_____

_____

___/___/20___

What will you do to celebrate yourself today?

_____

_____

_____

_____

___ /___ /20___

What are you an expert at?

_____

_____

_____

_____

___ /___ /20___

Who are three people you admire? Why do you admire them?

_____

_____

_____

_____

___ /___ /20___

What is your favorite activity on a rainy day?

_____

_____

_____

_____

___ /___ /20___

What are three things you would do if you weren't so afraid?

___ /___ /20___

What grand adventure do you wish you could go on?

___ /___ /20___

Where do you see yourself living in five years?

_____ / _____ / 20_____

What would you do if you could live a day without consequences?

_____

_____

_____

_____

_____ / _____ / 20_____

How do you unwind before bedtime?

_____

_____

_____

_____

_____ / _____ / 20_____

What home appliance do you appreciate most?

_____

_____

_____

_____

___ / ___ /20___

When is the last time you said 'thank you'?

_____

_____

_____

_____

___ / ___ /20___

What do you like most about yourself?

_____

_____

_____

_____

___ / ___ /20___

What in your life did you feel unbeatable?

_____

_____

_____

_____

_____ / _____ /20_____

What is your favorite museum?

_____

_____

_____

_____

_____ / _____ /20_____

What are you passionate about?

_____

_____

_____

_____

_____ / _____ /20_____

What three foods do you savor?

_____

_____

_____

_____

___ / ___ /20___

Who has your back?

_____

_____

_____

_____

___ / ___ /20___

Who in your life really needs your help?

_____

_____

_____

_____

___ / ___ /20___

What joke makes you laugh?

_____

_____

_____

_____

___ / ___ /20___

Who is the most enthusiastic person you know?

_____

_____

_____

_____

___ / ___ /20___

Who in your life are you thankful for?

_____

_____

_____

_____

___ / ___ /20___

What experience would you regret not having had?

_____

_____

_____

_____

___ / ___ / 20___

What would you do if you played hooky for a day?

_____

_____

_____

_____

___ / ___ / 20___

What is standing between you and happiness right now?

_____

_____

_____

_____

___ / ___ / 20___

What do you read for pleasure?

_____

_____

_____

_____ / _____ /20_____

If you were to go back to school, what would you study?

_____

_____

_____

_____

_____ / _____ /20_____

Who do you ask when you need an honest opinion?

_____

_____

_____

_____

_____ / _____ /20_____

What advice would you give to your teenage self?

_____

_____

_____

_____

___ / ___ /20___

What would you be willing to wait in line for?

___ / ___ /20___

What about you is worthy of admiration?

___ / ___ /20___

What makes you feel valued?

___ / ___ / 20 ___

What was better about today then yesterday?

_____

_____

_____

_____

___ / ___ / 20 ___

What are you going to accomplish in the next month?

_____

_____

_____

_____

___ / ___ / 20 ___

Finish the thought: The most positive thing I was part of is ...

_____

_____

_____

_____

___ / ___ /20___

When was a time when the impossible became possible?

_____

_____

_____

_____

___ / ___ /20___

What will you do for yourself this week?

_____

_____

_____

_____

___ / ___ /20___

What do you want the next chapter in your life to look like?

_____

_____

_____

_____

Made in the USA
Middletown, DE
03 December 2019